These poems belong to

....

From

....

Published by:
Candlestick Press, Diversity House, 72 Nottingham Road,
Arnold, Nottingham NG5 6LF

www.candlestickpress.co.uk

Design, typesetting, print and production by Diversity Creative
Marketing Solutions Ltd., diversitymarketing.co.uk

Illustrations © Amy Blackwell, 2013, amyblackwell.co.uk

© Candlestick Press, 2013

ISBN 978 1 907598 22 7

Acknowledgements:
Our thanks to the Literary Trustees of Walter de la Mare and
The Society of Authors as their representative for permission to
reproduce 'The Listeners' by Walter de la Mare from *The Listeners
and Other Poems* (Constable, 1912). Thanks are also due to the
Estate of Ian Serraillier for permission to reproduce 'The Visitor'
by Ian Serraillier, from *A Second Poetry Book*, edited by
John Foster (Oxford University Press, 1980) © Estate of
Ian Serraillier. 'Colonel Fazackerley' by Charles Causley is from
I Had a Little Cat – Collected Poems for Children (Macmillan
Children's Books, 1996). 'Timetable' by Julia Rawlinson is from
Read Me and Laugh: A Funny Poem for Every Day of the Year
(Macmillian Children's Books, 2005).

In a Dark Wood

In a dark, dark wood there was
    a dark, dark house,

And in that dark, dark house there was
    a dark, dark room,

And in that dark, dark room there was
    a dark, dark cupboard,

And in that dark, dark cupboard there was
    a dark, dark shelf,

And on that dark, dark shelf there was
    a dark, dark box,

And in that dark, dark box there was…

Anon

Colonel Fazackerley

Colonel Fazackerley Butterworth-Toast

Bought an old castle complete with a ghost,

But someone or other forgot to declare

To Colonel Fazack that the spectre was there.

On the very first evening, while waiting to dine,

The Colonel was taking a fine sherry wine,

When the ghost, with a furious flash and a flare,

Shot out of the chimney and shivered, 'Beware!'

Colonel Fazackerley put down his glass

And said, 'My dear fellow, that's really first class!

I just can't conceive how you do it at all.

I imagine you're going to a Fancy Dress Ball?'

At this, the dread ghost gave a withering cry.

Said the Colonel (his monocle firm in his eye),

'Now just how you do it I wish I could think.

Do sit down and tell me, and please have a drink.'

The ghost in his phosphorous cloak gave a roar

And floated about between ceiling and floor.

He walked through a wall and returned through a pane

And backed up the chimney and came down again.

Said the Colonel, 'With laughter I'm feeling quite weak!'

(As trickles of merriment ran down his cheek).

'My house-warming party I hope you won't spurn.

You must say you'll come and you'll give us a turn!'

At this, the poor spectre – quite out of his wits –

Proceeded to shake himself almost to bits.

He rattled his chains and he clattered his bones

And he filled the whole castle with mumbles and moans.

But Colonel Fazackerley, just as before,

Was simply delighted and called out, 'Encore!'

At which the ghost vanished, his efforts in vain,

And never was seen at the castle again.

'Oh dear, what a pity!' said Colonel Fazack.

'I don't know his name, so I can't call him back.'

And then with a smile that was hard to define,

Colonel Fazackerley went in to dine.

Charles Causley

The Visitor

A crumbling churchyard, the sea and the moon;

The waves had gouged out grave and bone;

A man was walking, late and alone…

He saw a skeleton on the ground;

A ring on a bony finger he found.

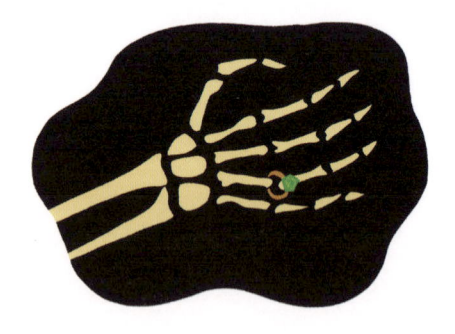

He ran home to his wife and gave her the ring.

'Oh, where did you get it?' He said not a thing.

'It's the loveliest ring in the world,' she said,

As it glowed on her finger. They slipped off to bed.

At midnight they woke. In the dark outside,

'Give me my ring!' a chill voice cried.

'What was that, William? What did it say?'

'Don't worry, my dear. It'll soon go away.'

'I'm coming!' A skeleton opened the door.

'Give me my ring!' It was crossing the floor.

'What was that, William? What did it say?'

'Don't worry, my dear. It'll soon go away.'

'I'm reaching you now! I'm climbing the bed.'

The wife pulled the sheet right over her head.

It was torn from her grasp and tossed in the air:

'I'll drag you out of your bed by the hair!'

'What was that, William? What did it say?'

'Throw the ring through the window!
                              THROW IT AWAY!'

She threw it. The skeleton leapt from the sill,

Scooped up the ring and clattered downhill,

Fainter…and fainter…Then all was still.

Ian Serraillier

The Listeners

'Is there anybody there?' said the Traveller,
    Knocking on the moonlit door;
And his horse in the silence champed the grasses
    Of the forest's ferny floor:

And a bird flew up out of the turret,
    Above the Traveller's head:
And he smote upon the door again a second time;
    'Is there anybody there?' he said.

But no one descended to the Traveller;
    No head from the leaf-fringed sill
Leaned over and looked into his grey eyes,
    Where he stood perplexed and still.
But only a host of phantom listeners
    That dwelt in the lone house then
Stood listening in the quiet of the moonlight
    To that voice from the world of men:
Stood thronging the faint moonbeams on the dark stair,
    That goes down to the empty hall,
Hearkening in an air stirred and shaken
    By the lonely Traveller's call.
And he felt in his heart their strangeness,
    Their stillness, answering his cry,
While his horse moved, cropping the dark turf,
    'Neath the starred and leafy sky;

For he suddenly smote on the door, even
    Louder, and lifted his head:-
'Tell them I came, and no one answered,
    That I kept my word,' he said.

Never the least stir made the listeners,
    Though every word he spake
Fell echoing through the shadowiness of the still house
    From the one man left awake:
Ay, they heard his foot upon the stirrup,
    And the sound of iron on stone,
And how the silence surged softly backward,
    When the plunging hoofs were gone.

Walter de la Mare

Timetable

First-year ghosts, 9 p.m.,
First class, 'Elementary Moaning,'
10 p.m. at local churchyard,
'Get to Grips with Graveyard Groaning,'
10.30, practical,
'How to Remove your Head,'
12 midnight, back to churchyard,
'Seven Steps to Wake the Dead,'
1 a.m., 'Dragging Chains,'
2 a.m., 'Ringing Bells,'
3 a.m., 'To Mix Fake Blood,'
4 a.m., 'Revolting Smells,'
5 a.m., dawn instructions,
'Murky Mists and Spooky Lighting,'
5.30, theory class,
'The Basics of Successful Frightening,'
6 a.m., lost property,
Please reclaim your missing head,
6.30, class dismissed,
Vanish, fade or float to bed.

Julia Rawlinson

Now it's your turn to write a poem about a gh...gh...ghost or draw a picture of one!